The New Cosmic Order
A Travellers Guide

Peter ben Yusuf

The Universal Information Station
A Myrrhidian Channel

For One and All,
For All as One
For each individual One in The All

The New Cosmic Order
A Tale Worth Digesting

Other titles by Peter ben Yusuf

The Fifth Dimension – A Prime All

The Thirteenth Moon – A Sea Quell

The Atlantean – Triumphant

The Meta Theorem

Unicornia

www.peterbenyusuf.blogspot.com.au

Contents

Science

Physics is the Universal Science
Mathematics is the Universal Language

Let No One Ignorant of Geometry Enter Here - Plato

Maths and Geometry are the only Exact Sciences.
Harmony in the Mathematical World of sense is
Justice in the World of Spirit.

All science stems from Physics.

Physics is the application of Mathematics

Engineering is the application of Physics to the Physical.

Botany is the application of Physics to the Botanical

Physiology is the application of Physics to the Physiological.

Geophysics is the application of Physics to the Geological.

Cosmology is the application of Physics to the Astronomical.

Laws of physics are by nature multidimensional, as there are as many observer's as there are souls.
Self-Righteous is not Righteousness itself,

Meta physics is not separate from the physics, it is after the physics.

Hypothesis (An idea that can be tested)

It appears that Energy affects our reality and what we put into the atmosphere, physically and energetically, affects the Earth that supports us. Nature balances out the differences in accordance with the laws of Creation. It appears that mass and energy exist simultaneously physically and physiologically and thus the four dimensional law of conservation works two ways in a five dimensional reality, conserving mass and energy in a Natural harmonious balance. It also appears that not only do mass and energy physically exist simultaneously as evidenced by molecular, electronic devices and machines. It also appears that mass and energy co-exist in a variety of organisms (Biological) and Physiological beings as well.

The Laws of physics are relative to the observer.

It all began in the beginning…
Until I existed in physiological form The Universe was
unobservable from a human perspective.
It was incomprehensible until I understood the means
utilised to define that which was questioned.

The First Dimension

One Dimensional - Length; A line, Linear.

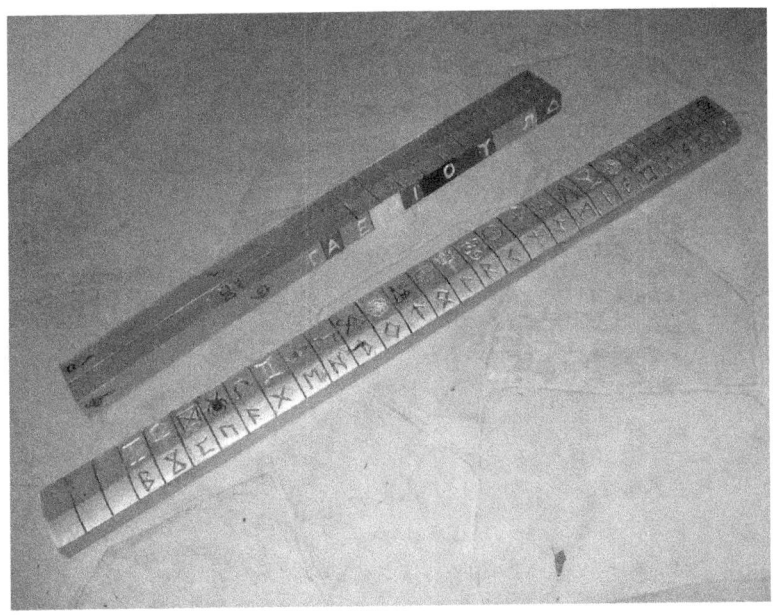

The Vertical Plane: Up and down, Height
The Horizontal Plane: Left and Right, Width
The Perceptual Plane: Forward and back, Depth;

The Second Dimension

Two Dimensional: Area; A Plane, A Surface, A Field.

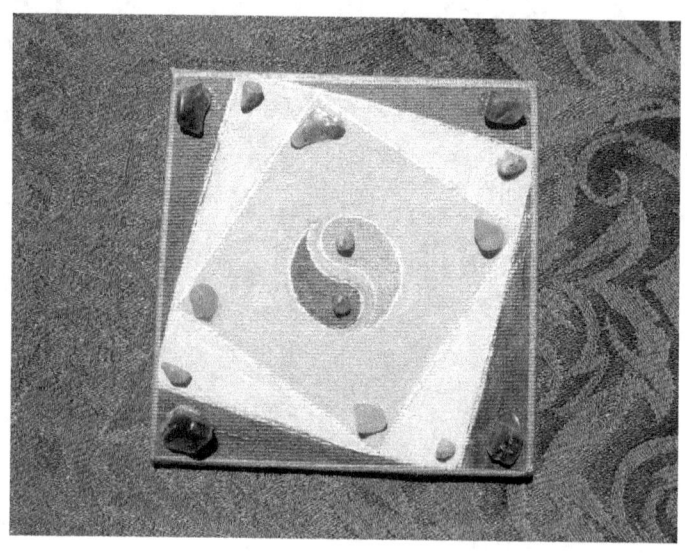

Height by Width
Or Width by Depth
Or Height by Depth

The Third Dimension

Three Dimensional

Volume: Occupies Space; A Cube, A Sphere, A Body
Height by Width by Depth

Units of Measure

Scale, Proportion, Balance

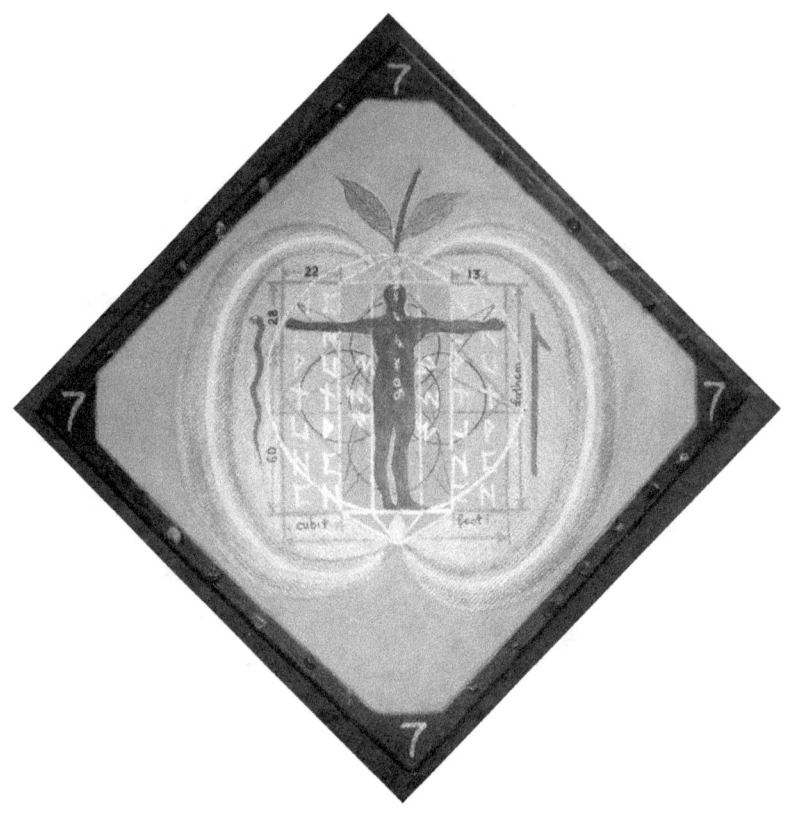

| 7 x 7 = 49 |
| 7 x 4 = 28 |

The pendulum swing to the Left

Is the pendulum swing to the Right

Fractions

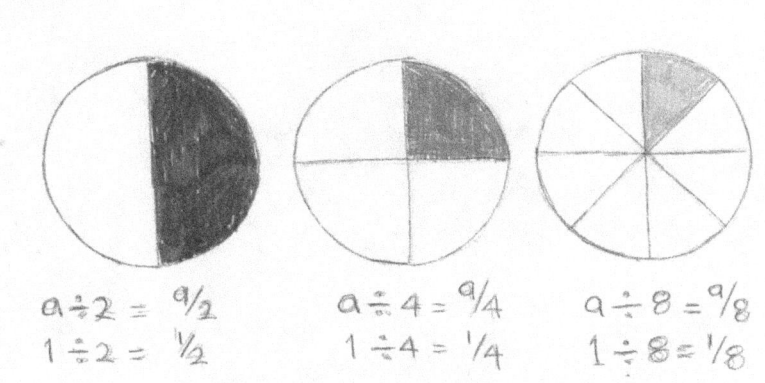

$$a \div 2 = \frac{a}{2}$$
$$1 \div 2 = \frac{1}{2}$$

$$a \div 4 = \frac{a}{4}$$
$$1 \div 4 = \frac{1}{4}$$

$$a \div 8 = \frac{a}{8}$$
$$1 \div 8 = \frac{1}{8}$$

The part is contained in the whole
The whole is the sum of all the parts
The part is not the whole
The whole is not the part.
The All Encompassing Tao is All Encompassing

Binary by power

1, 2, 4, 8, 16, 32, 64

Binary by Progression
1, 1, 2, 3, 5, 8, 13, 21, 34, 55, 89, 144

Algebra

$$6 + \square = 10$$
$$6 + a = 10$$
$$a = \square$$

$$5 - \square = 2$$
$$5 - a = 2$$
$$a = \square$$

$$5 \times \square = 10$$
$$5 \times a = 10$$
$$5a = 10$$
$$a = \square$$

$$4/\square = 2$$
$$4/a = 2$$
$$4 \text{ divided by } a = 2$$
$$a = \square$$

$$a/2 + 6 = 12$$
$$a/2 + 6 - 6 = 12 - 6$$
$$a/2 = 6$$
$$a/2 \times 2 = 6 \times 2$$
$$a = 12$$

Quantification

Quantification pertains to area $a \times a = a^2$

To quantify a length of 7 units of measure

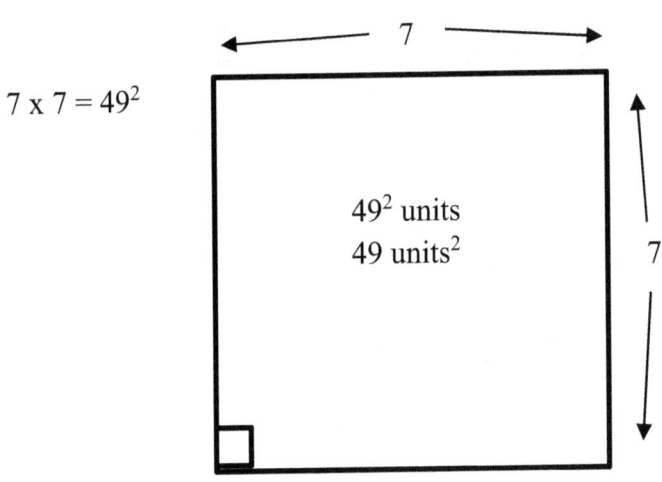

$7 \times 7 = 49^2$

49^2 units

49 units^2

A Point is where two lines intersect

Pythagoras' Theorem

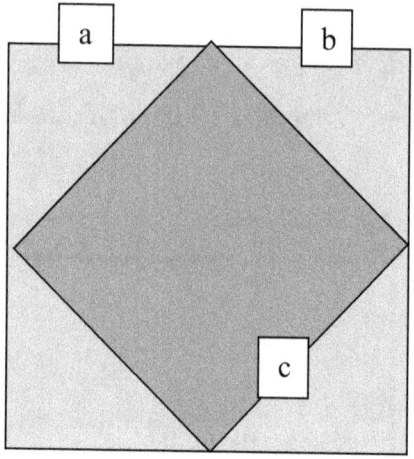

A square with a value of a + b squared
is equal to 4 triangles ab plus the centre square

$$(a + b)^2 = 4(^1/_2ab) + c^2$$

In its expanded form

$$a^2 + 2ab + b^2 = 2ab + c^2$$

$$a^2 + 2ab (-2ab) + b^2 = 2ab (-2ab) + c^2$$

In its reduced form

$$a^2 + b^2 = c^2$$

Matter, Mass, Energy

Properties of matter;
Matter is anything that has a molecular structure and
occupies space.
Matter exists in 3 states of being, solid liquid and gas
Matter contains mass, therefore it must and always will
generate mass as it changes between states.

Energy and its forms being the fourth state of being.
Energy is the ability to do work.
Energy has no molecular structure, Temperature, Pressure,
Velocity.
An Electromagnetic Field is mass in a conserved state.
Electromagnetic Fluidity requires mass (magnet) and Energy
(a flow of electrons) to appear.

Galea; 5 dimensional Physics.
Mass exists (3D volume), Energy exists (2D Field).
Mass and energy co-exist within and express itself from a
physical form.
Life is observed from and reliant upon interaction with the
totality of the Universal Environment.

Defining a point

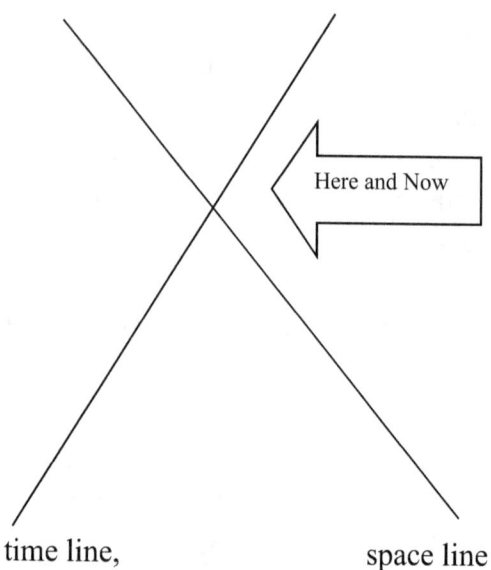

time line,   space line

A point is where two lines intersect.

Euclidean Calculus is based on One Plane of Observable Existance; Two Dimensional

Triangulation

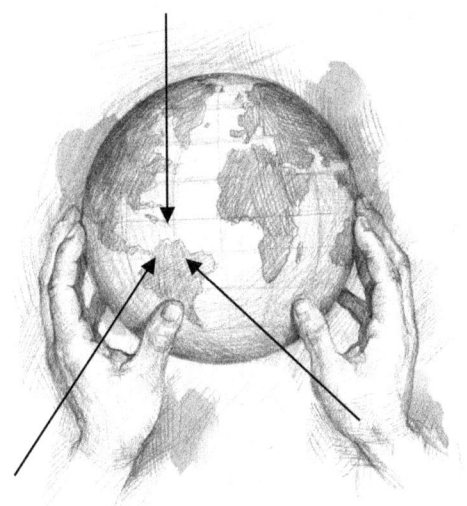

Triangulation; c is relative to 3 points.

Newtonian Calculus is based on Three Planes of
Observable Existance. Three Dimensional

The Fourth Dimension

$E = mc^2$; Energy is equal to mass multiplied by the speed of light squared.

Conservation;

That matter and Energy are but different manifestations of the same substance.

From this perspective Energy appears as a 2 dimensional field and mass appears three dimensional as it occupies space with a volume of mass.

Constant; The linear speed of light, travelling in a straight line one dimensionally, is constant relative to the speed of a two dimensional electromagnetic field.

Electromagnetic Fluidity radiates at phi and the linear speed of light travels at the square root of phi they appear constant relative to one another.

Energy as 2 dimensional field; $E=m\phi$

Light appears as a particle (linear) and wave (field) and are constant relative to one another.

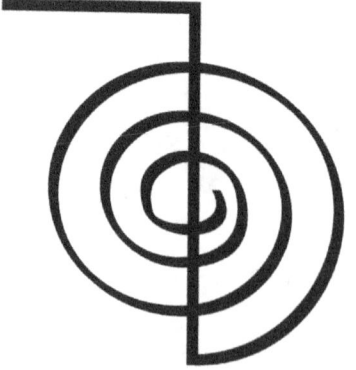

$$c = \sqrt{\phi}$$
$$c^2 = \phi$$
$$E = m\phi$$

The Fifth Dimension

If mass is measured as three dimensional and an energy field is measured as two dimensional,
The union of Mass and Energy, such as Plasma, appears five dimensional. 3D + 2D = 5D

> Yin can be Yang
> Yang can be Yin
> Yin cannot be without Yang
> Yang cannot be without Yin
> Yin and Yang create the Tao

Natural Balance

Time, Space and Place

TVM; Time, Volume, Mass. Time is the observation of mass moving relative to other masses occupying a volume of space;

Cosmology is where Astrology and Astronomy align.

The motions and location of the Sun, Moon, the Stars relative to the observer.

Duration and Measure observe movements that are occurring two dimensionally on a plane, and three dimensionally in a volume of space.

The shortest distance between two points is a straight line.

$s = d/t$, speed equals distance divided by time;

The measured distance between two objects divided by the time travelled is equal to the objects speed.

The measured distance between two objects divided by the objects speed is equal to the time travelled.

Therefore time is simply distance divided by speed. $t = d/s$.

Universal Time is always "Now" for all observers

Cosmic Time is based on Cosmology.
Planetery Time is relative to the observers planetary location "Here"

Naturally True, Physically True, Universally True.

Definition of Time

The closest we can become to observing time is by what the Buddhist call "being time". The best description of the word is "Here and Now", the moment of awareness. Things move but time stands still. When we say that time passes, what is really happening is that we pass through time.

When we say we observe time, we are actually observing the passing of our minds, the movement of our thought process. Time itself has nothing to do with Past, Present, and Future. These are events in time, not time itself.

I Am That I Am

A life without mystery would be like a heart without love,
...and where would we be without love?

I am a mystery, and so it seems.
I do respect the power of dreams
The dream of the Buddha, the dream of the Son
Are they not just expressions of love?
The dream of the Krishna of prophets that come
Are they not all visions of the love of the dove?
To show unto you what science does smother
Is what I am hoping that you will discover
To challenge the intellect, to enhance your desire,
I do hope my words do lift you higher
Higher in wisdom, in love and good faith,
Perhaps I can show you the love of the wraith
Love one another is what has been said,
How hard is that to get in our heads?
I am not perfect I am just a man,
I am as I seem, I am that I am
If prophecy is fulfilled for that I am glad,
The situation on Earth does make me sad
What of the children, generations to come,
Are we all relying on the flight of the dove?
It is up to us collectively to make the change,
One man cannot do it, are you insane
They call me delusional and so it seems,
Because I respect the power of dreams
The future of life is what I respect,

Is that really too much to expect?
If all is conserved we will live again,
Unless all we do is dream in vain
Respect one another; the Earth is our home,
Why do I feel I stand all alone?
What of the children, the future race?
Is it all left up to God's Grace?
The evidence is there in front of our eyes,
Why are we all so desperate to hide?
The truth of the matter that can't be denied,
It is hidden, diverted, covered with lies
Stand up and be counted, don't be afraid.
The Earth will thank you, tenfold it is said.
Stand firm in your faith, Earth Mother she cares.
Am I to be the only one who dares?
To challenge the system that is bringing us down,
I do wish to be here, to hang around
To alter the future, for better of course,
With my faith behind me upon a white horse
I am that I am, I know what is real,
We can achieve a better deal
I dream in the day, perhaps you dream at night.
Does it really matter who is more right.
I am not perfect, I am just a man, I am as I seem,
I am that I am

The Energy Trinity
Force through a magnet produces Energy.
Energy through a magnet produces Force.

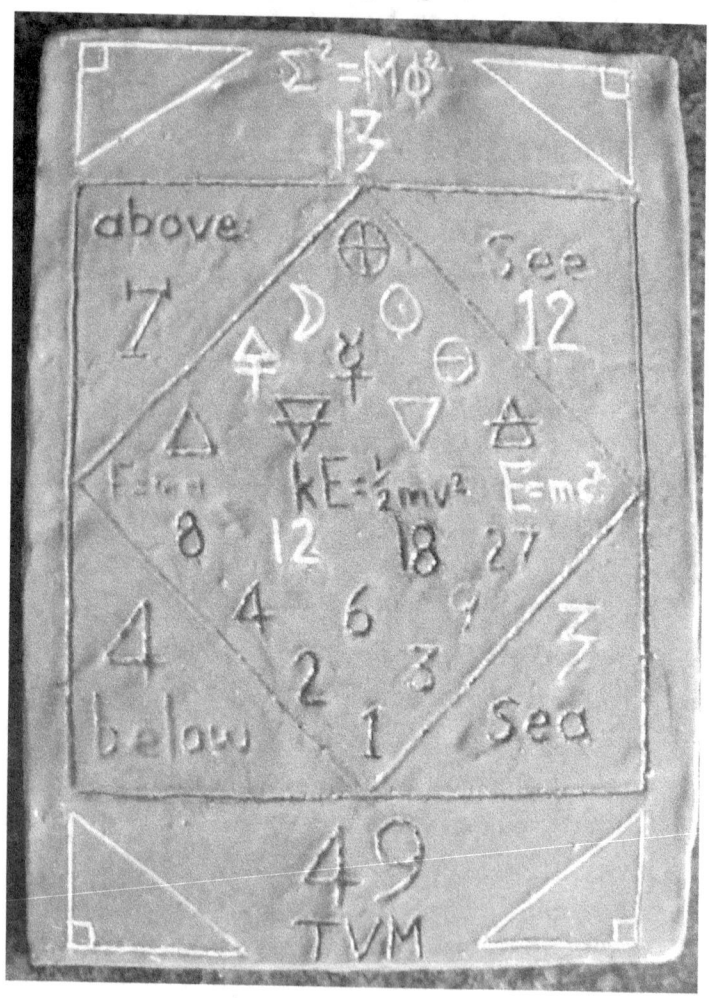

The Clay tablet of Peter the Atlantean

The Meta theorem; $E^2 = M\Phi^2$

Galea; Energy as three dimensional; $E^2=M\phi^2$

An Energy Field is quantifiable and flowing as a Torus is equal to solid mass, liquid mass and gaseous mass

$3D \times 3 = M=m^2$

Existing in time and space, ϕ, observed from time and space,+1.

$\phi+1 = \phi^2$

Everything exists in three states relative to temperature, pressure and velocity (Energy, the fourth State)

Reconciling the Calendars

A Planetary Day

As the Earth orbits its centre, the Zodiac revolves approximately one revolution, 360 degrees, per day, 15 degrees per hour.

A Solar Year

As the Earth orbits the Sun, the Zodiac revolves 360 degrees per year, 30 degrees per month.

A Cosmic Year

As the Sun orbits Galactic Central Point, the Zodiac revolves at one degree every seventy two years.

$72 \times 360 = 25,920$

A Cosmic Month, of 30 degrees, is equal to 2160 solar years.

$30 \times 72 = 2160$

$2160 \times 12 = 25920$

Experimental Evidence that the Sun Orbits the Galaxy:

Galileo observed the orbital patterns of Jupiter's moons in alignment with the Galactic Field. He successfully applied the same principal to the Earth's orbit about the Sun which explained the seasonal changes and subsequent Solstices and Equinoxes. Copernicus also observed that all the Planets, wandering stars, orbit the Sun and thus the path of the Planets follow the path that the Sun follows.
The Solar Calendar is based upon these findings.

Muslim, Jewish and Chinese calendar's incorporate the Lunar Cycles and it is between these orbital patterns (the Earth's orbit about the Sun, and the Moons orbit about the Earth) that Solar and Lunar Eclipses can be predetermined with mathematical precision and accuracy.

The Earth's seasons, the solstices and equinoxes are in accord with the Earth's orbit around the Sun. The moons rising is fixed in the East, whilst the Sun rise shifts along the horizon from summer to winter due to the Earths orbital pattern.

In applying the same principal discovered by Galileo to the Suns Orbit around Galactic Central Point the precession of the Equinoxes are also observed, calculated and may be predetermined relative to the fixed stars and wandering stars.

The Earth's orbit around the Sun relative to Galactic centre and the gravitational influences applied are what affects Elliptical orbits and the harmony of the spheres as discovered by Kepler.

Cosmology;

Perspective and the astronomical perspectives contained therein. (Helios, centripetal and centrifugal forces).

The Geomagnetic model also honours the Energy Trinity and the composition of Plasma (containing both mass and Energy) Physical, Physiological and Geophysical.

5D Gravity; Geomagnetism

The link between Mass, Gravity and Magnetism

The geomagnetic fields and vortices that operate around and between bodies of mass hold bodies in harmonious orbit about each other and in symphony with the galactic field. That the Centripetal and centrifugal forces that govern the Earth's orbit around the Sun apply in an equal and opposite fashion between the Sun and Galactic Central Point.

Newton – Bodies are attracted to each other in a direct relationship with their mass and an inverse relationship to the square of their distances

Kepler's third law – The squares of the periods of revolution of any two Planets are as cubes of their mean distance from the Sun.

Galea; 5D Geomagnetic Gravity –

Bodies of mass are attracted to each other in a direct relationship with their mass (centripetal) and an inverse relationship to the square of their distances (centrifugal). This is due to the magnetic influence caused by the sum total of electrons accumulated in each body of mass.

Proton Vortice and Pole

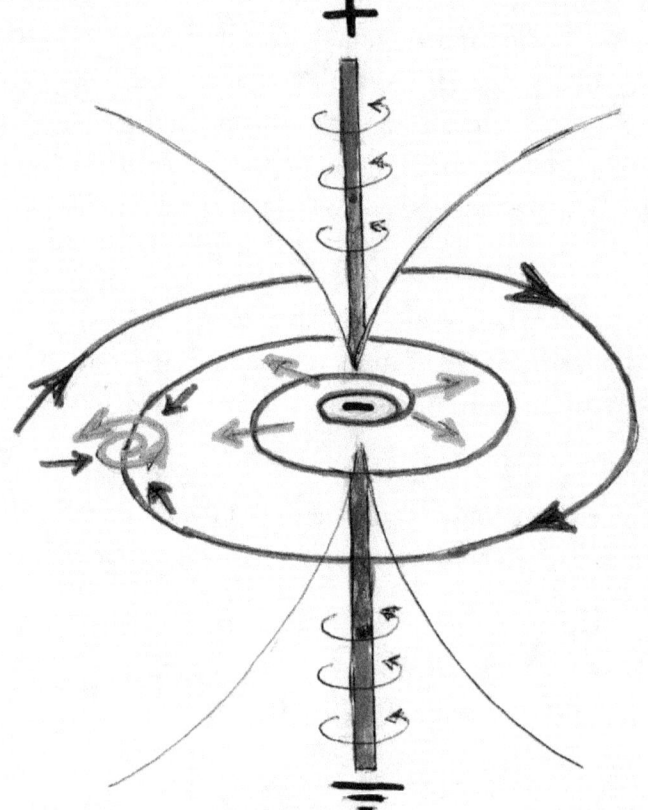

Nuetron Vortice and Pole

Galactic Structure and Function

Centripetal and Centrifugal forces.

Toroidal flow of Gravity

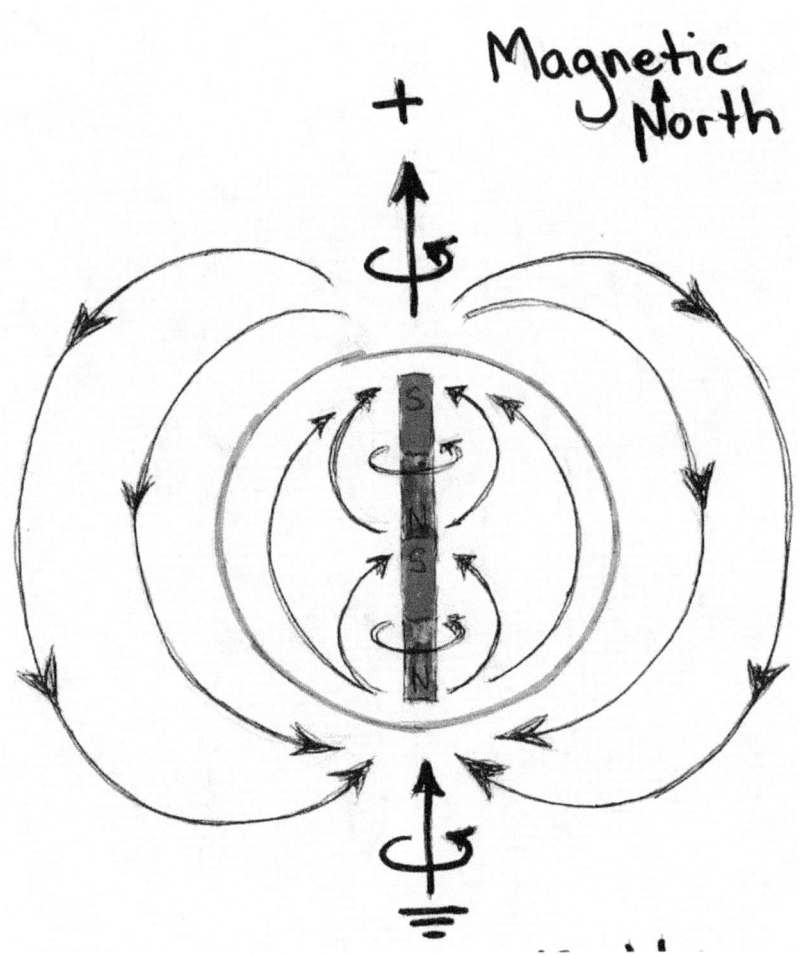

Two opposite poles attract

Solar Centre

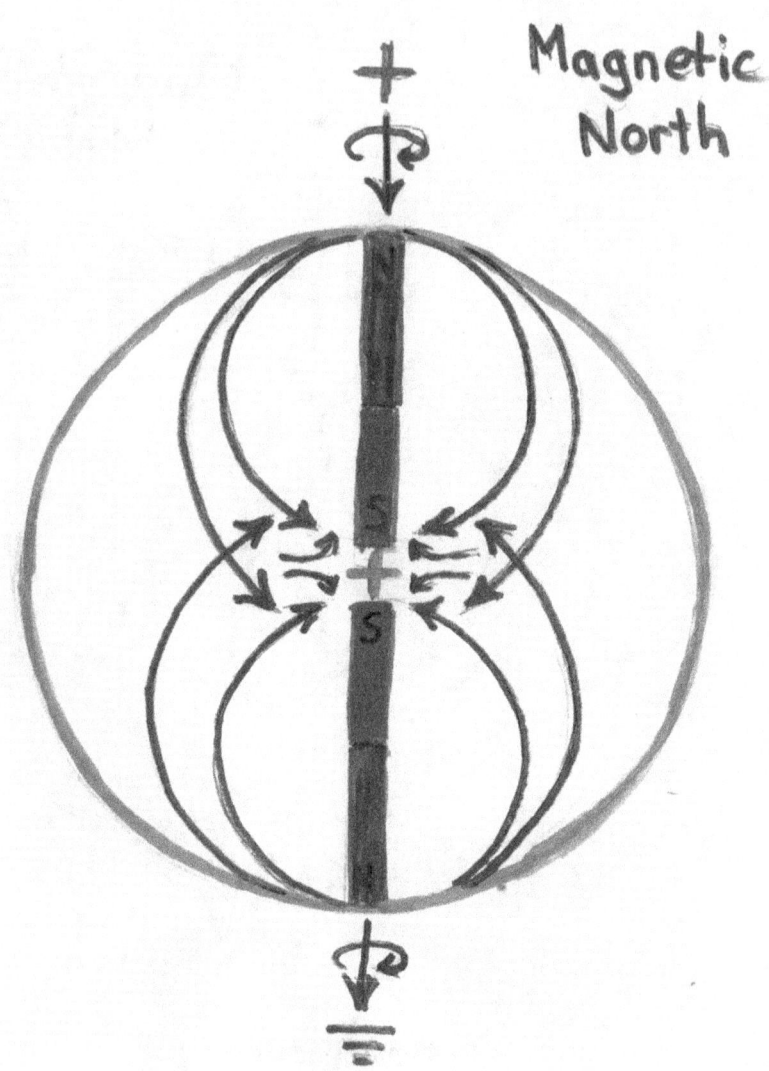

Two similar poles oppose

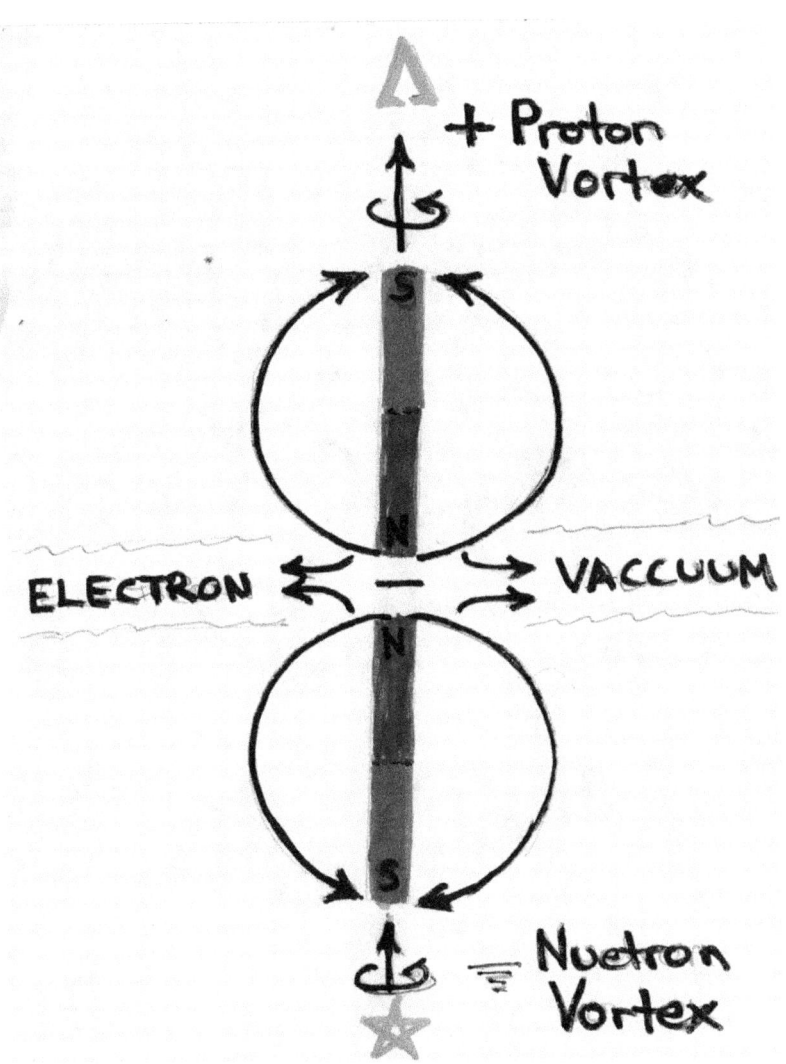

Two similar poles oppose

Toroidal Structure of Galaxy

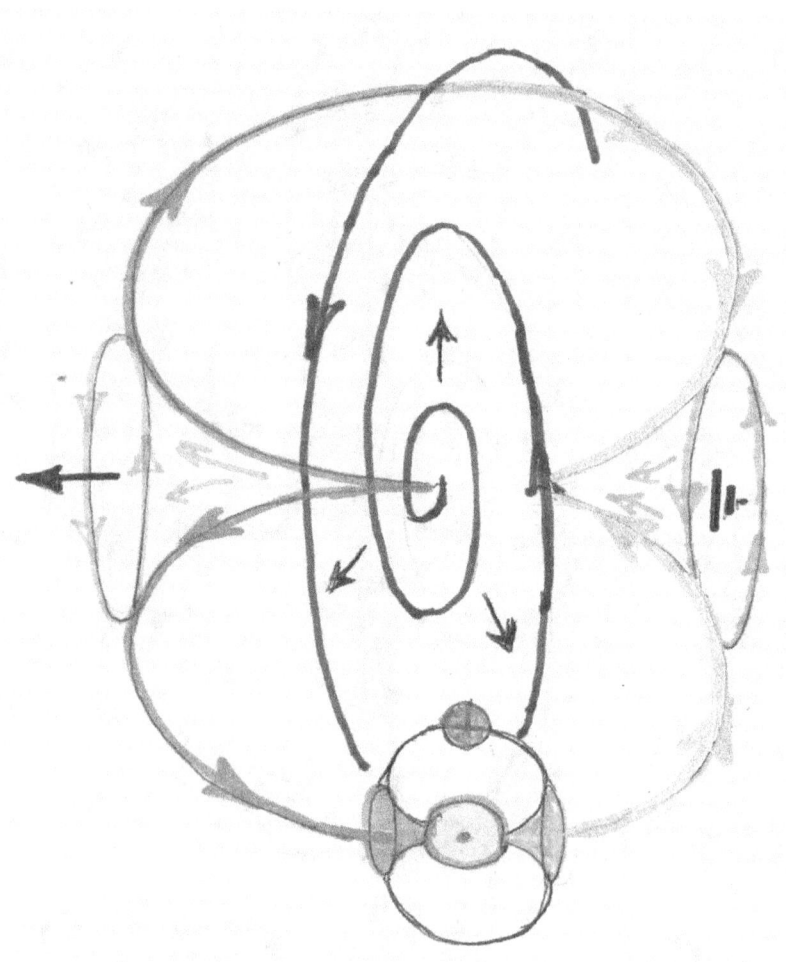

North Poles

South Poles

Galactic Field

Galactic Geomagnetic Schematic

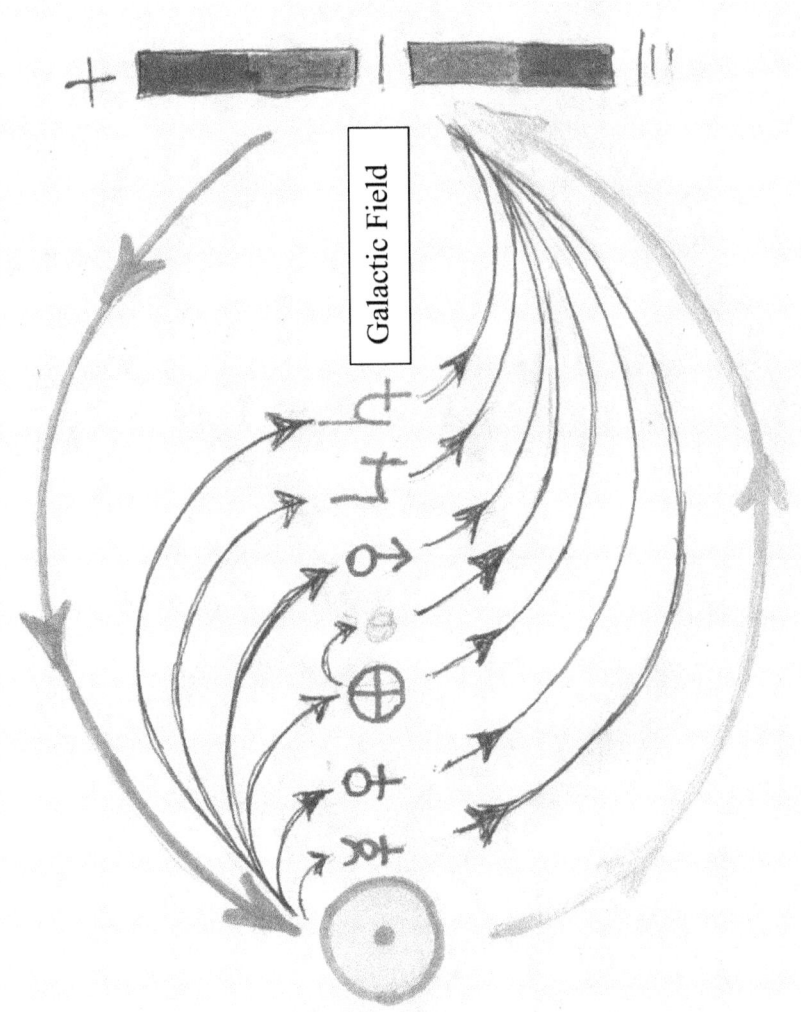

Flow of Energy maintains polar alignment in the Galactic Field

Geomagnetic Fluidity

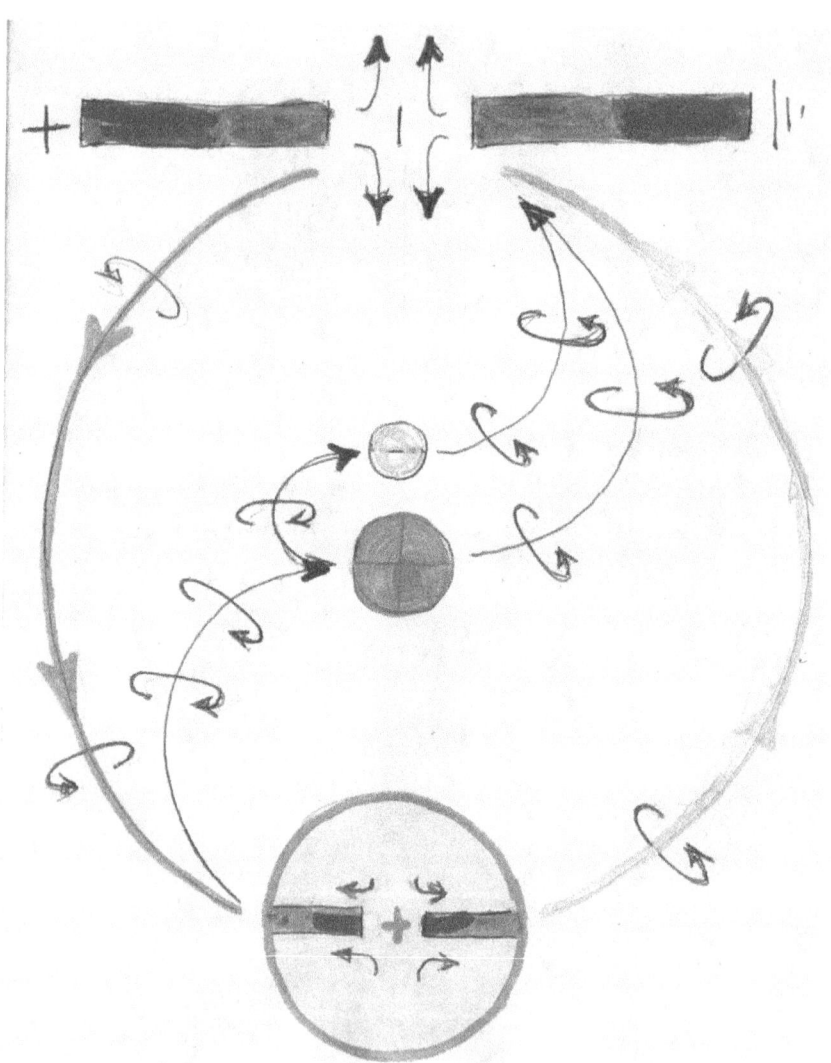

Toroidal flow of Gravity maintains polar spin

Galea; Orbit of Direct Proportion-

The Square of the periods of revolution of any two bodies of Mass in orbit are as the cube of the mean distance from their orbital central Mass.

Whether it be the moons orbit about the Earth;

The Earth's orbit about the Sun;

The Suns orbit about the Galaxy;

The Galaxies orbit about the Cosmos existing between two relative fields.

Galea; Kinetic Velocity; $kV = V^3/2\Phi$

The velocity of a body in motion is equal to its velocity cubed existing between two relative fields.

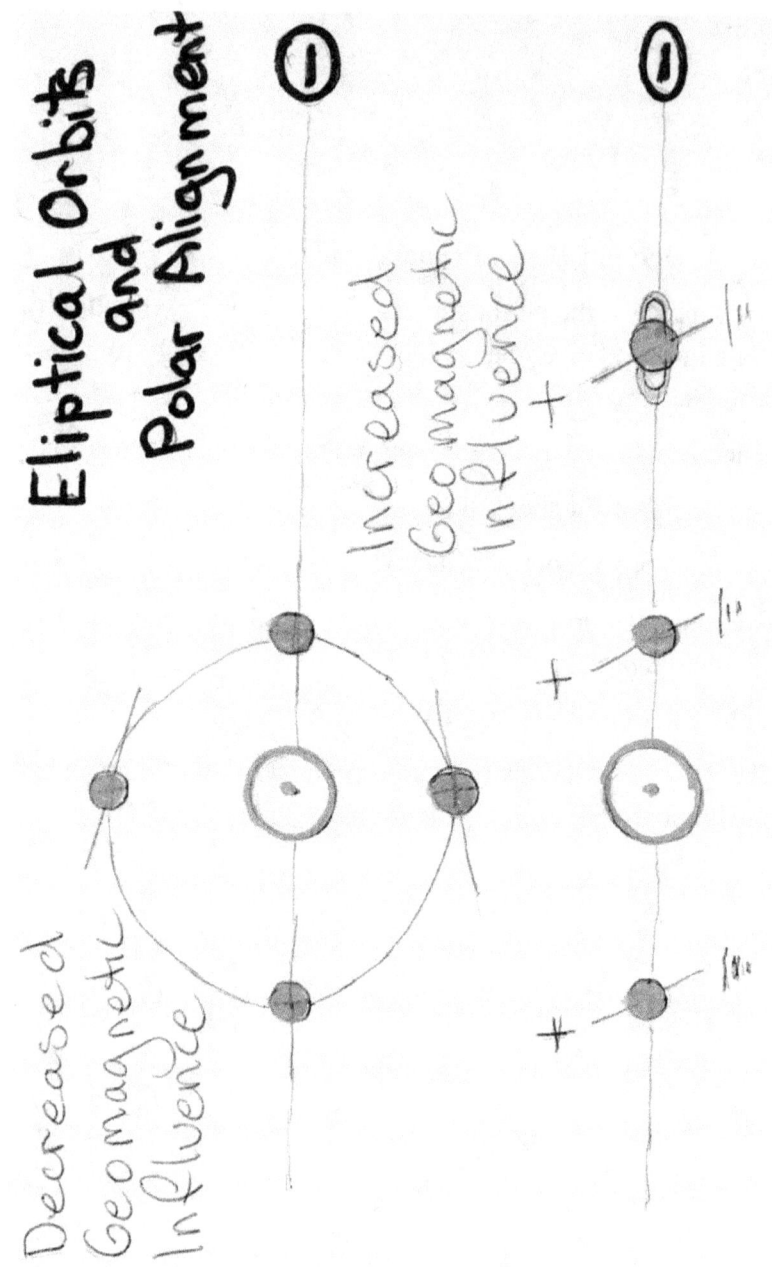

Eliptical Orbits and Polar Alignment

Decreased Geomagnetic Influence

Increased Geomagnetic Influence

48

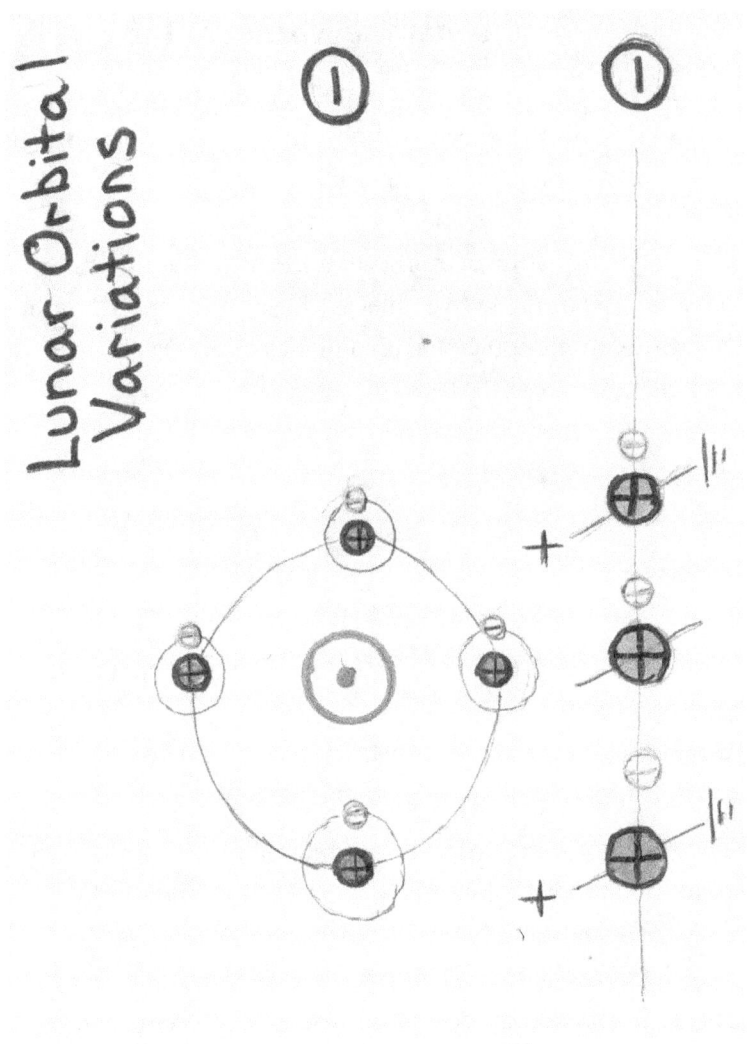

The Lunar Perigee is due to Forces in the Galactic Field between the Sun, the Moon and Galactic Central Point.

Optics and the Nature of Light

As the linear, one dimensional, speed of light exists in harmony with the speed of light utilising the field of vision, two dimensionally, the linear and peripheral visions may be combined to add depth to vision and objects viewed three dimensionally still retaining their clear and vivid appearance as well as coloured hue due to these light speed variances being directly proportional on 3 planes of observable existence as light emanates.

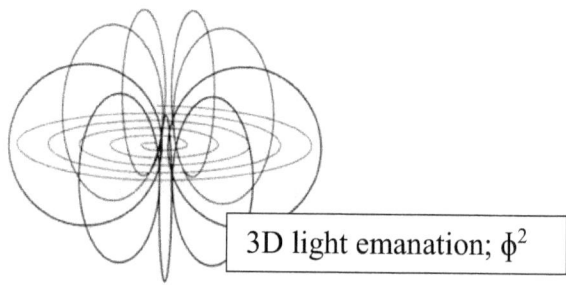

3D light emanation; ϕ^2

E = mϕ; light travels as a particle (linear) and wave (field) and are constant relative to one another.

The speed of light existing as c^2 maintains a two dimensional field of vision which if represented by the ratio of phi, ϕ, is directly proportional to the linear aspect of the speed of light calculated as the inverse of phi, $\sqrt{\phi}$, to represent linear light speed. Likewise the ratio of phi squared, ϕ^2, representing the three dimensional speed of light maintains relative frequency and speed from a multidimensional perspective as the linear speed of light is directly proportional to an emanation of light. Harmonising linear vision with the field of vision while maintaining clarity and depth regardless of the image observed.

Neptunian Man

Neptunian man, how does he see?

With his eyes, with his mind or consciously

Can he count, does he fathom, is what he says true

Has he included himself in the equation there too?

Has he counted the Angels and the Faeries as well?

Has he counted the souls that are going through hell?

Has he counted the elementals?

The birds and the bees

Has he counted the flowers, the shrubs and trees?

Has he counted the waves as well as the stars?

What is it he sees, how deep and how far?

Has he counted the Creator as part of the seas?

Has he measured the foot up to the knee?

Or has he just counted between you and me?

Was he there at the start as well as the end?

Was he the rooster that made the chicken a hen?

Has he counted the heartbeat

Of the Earth's crystalline core?

Did he pass through the ethers

And knock on deaths door?

Does he dream of the Dai is he a wake in the Knight?

Is he the one that measured the light?

Neptunian man, how does he see?

With his eyes, with his mind or consciously

The Field of Dreams

The Old Ones say that at one time all of Creation spoke the same language. The plants could communicate with the finned ones, the four-leggeds could speak with the trees, the stones could talk with the wind, and even the most dependent part of creation, the two-leggeds, or as we have come to call ourselves, the humans, could also speak with the other parts of creation. All existed in harmony. The plants, the animals, and the elements of the Four Directions (all existence) all knew that if the two-leggeds were to survive, they would need help.

The Earth as a Chrysalises

Before all things it is necessary to have a right understanding of nature. It originates from divine virtue.

Looking within the Global environment the four states of being may be observed. The Earth itself is made of various solid compounds such as rocks and metals, liquid exist in various forms from lava, molten rock to fresh water ponds, rivers and lakes which flow to the salt water seas and oceans. The air we breathe is of a gaseous nature as well as various other gasses venting into the atmosphere through various avenues. Fire exists spontaneously as combustion, as well as static electricity created by friction unto electricity caused by lightning strikes.

The various states of being of matter exist in their state relative to temperature, pressure and velocity applied to them and forces acting upon them which is maintained by the environment in its natural state to maintain equilibrium, Geo-stasis and sustain geo magnetic fields, grids and flow.

Earth and its environment appears as a living entity, as a chrysalis for consciousness evolution, an environment for experiencing and learning many and various aspects of nature with all four states of being existing simultaneously in a state of regeneration. Each aspect affecting another aspect as all is held firmly within the Earth's atmosphere maintained by the balance and cycles of nature contained within the vessel and each aspect of change in turn affecting other parts of the chrysalises.

Four atoms create a molecule (tetrabasic) molecules in turn create compounds, solutions and gases. Atoms and molecules exist in cellular structures, organisms and it is within structures which life is contained.

Metaphysics is not separate from the physics, it is after the Physics

Meta Essence is the life force of wonderland.

The Laws of
Physics are relative
to the observer

The Physical World
is relative to you!

Peter ben Yusuf

As above, so below
As without, so within

An Holistic Approach

Health and All Heal.

Can you place a healthy being in an unhealthy environment
and expect them to retain their core health?

Integrative health

One of the reasons humans struggle to heal and are living in
pain and discomfort is because they are trying to manage the
symptoms when they could be healing the cause or trigger of
their problems. For a person to truly heal and experience
health, harmony and vitality they need to aim for a holistic
approach, integrating themselves in harmony with natural
balance.

Homeostasis is The Natural Balance that is maintained by
biological flow.

Biology and Psyche of the Human Being exists within the
Global Environment. Naturally occurring Cycles and
frequencies of the environment are also regulated by Natural
Laws.

The Laws of Physics are Universal,
They apply equally indiscriminately without condition.
Love has no conditions

Elements – States of Being

Everything exists in four states of being,

Solid – Earth
Liquid – Water
Gas – Air
Energy – Fire

Elementals were first described in the 1600's CE by noted German Physician and Alchemist Paracelsus; he is considered the Father of Homeopathy.

The Familiar Trinity

We created you from a single pair.
Mother, Father and Child

Genetic Evolution;
Each Individual was Created from a single Pair.

Social Evolution;
Each Individual is part of a Global Society.

Consciousness Evolution;
Each individual has the ability to think for themselves

No two sets of eyes can see the same rainbow,
No two people can occupy the same space at the same
time.

Aristotles Triangle
Pathos; Appeals to the emotion
Ethos; Making an ethical choice
Logos; Facts and data

3 Planes of observable existence
7 Directions

Balance

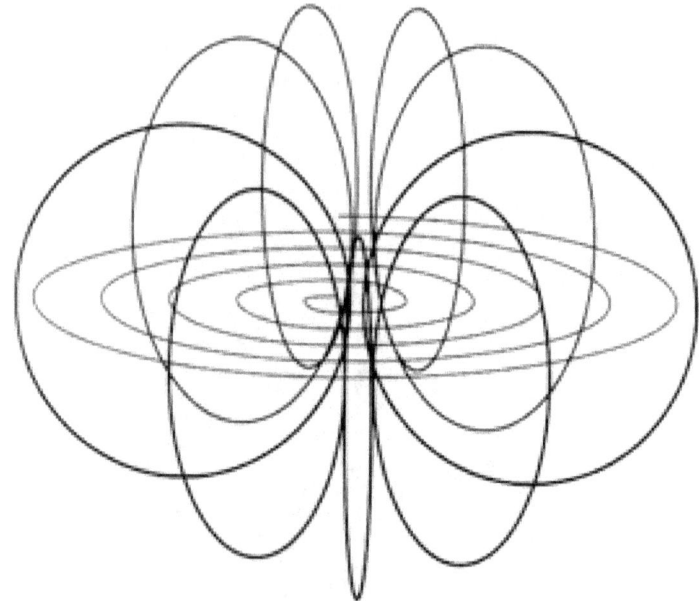

Figure 3: 7D Galactic Photon Bands

Global Consciousness –

All of Creation exists together as One.

Each individual aspects of creation is required for All to be as One.

The Isness Is! If it is not, then so it is.

5 Dimensional Psi Key; Ψ

Left and Right Brain Unity Consciousness; 3D +2D = 5D

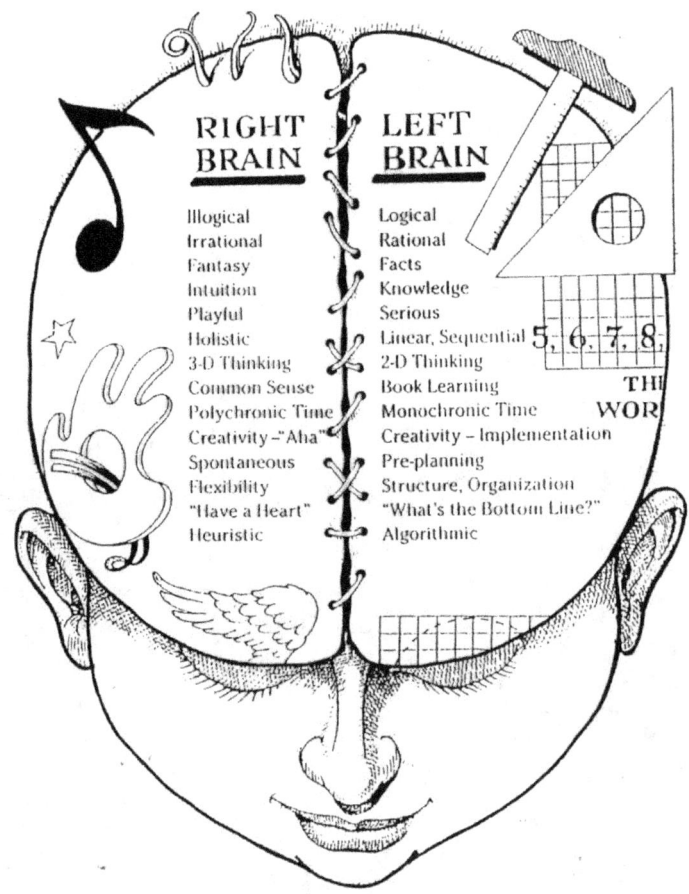

RIGHT BRAIN

Illogical
Irrational
Fantasy
Intuition
Playful
Holistic
3-D Thinking
Common Sense
Polychronic Time
Creativity –"Aha"
Spontaneous
Flexibility
"Have a Heart"
Heuristic

LEFT BRAIN

Logical
Rational
Facts
Knowledge
Serious
Linear, Sequential
2-D Thinking
Book Learning
Monochronic Time
Creativity – Implementation
Pre-planning
Structure, Organization
"What's the Bottom Line?"
Algorithmic

Psychonomy;

The word that is written and the mind that interprets it.

The Gamma and the Delta

Five Frequencies to Understanding

Humans display five different types of electrical patterns or "brain waves" across the cortex.

Gamma, Beta, Alpha, Theta, and Delta

These brain waves which have no molecular or cellular structure of their own can be observed with an EEG (electroencephalograph). Each brain wave serves a purpose and helps serve in consciousness awareness.

A mental body that becomes an instrument not a master

To become aware of the five senses, and then couple discrimination with dispassion, the highest spirit and the lowest matter linked together by intelligence. This combines to provide us with True Nature, Intuition, and Intelligence.

The threefold nature of

Intelligence, Love, and Divine will.

An Interactive Hieroglyphic Universe

Thought is idle until it manifests with word, sign or symbol.

The basis of absolute hieroglyphical science was an alphabet in which deities were represented by letters, letters represented ideas, ideas were convertible into number and numbers equate to perfects signs.

Hieroglyphics is the signs of number, ideas and forms in their sacred alphabet. Cuneiform is embedded in many written languages and gem atria is encoded within as numerical expression.

Mathematics is the Universal Language.

The world is arranged according to mathematical laws.

The harmony of geometrics and mathematics are the only exact sciences. Harmony in the physical and mathematical world of sense is justice in the spiritual one.

Topology is symbolic of matrices yet cannot define the matrix itself. Number has Cosmic significance, astrologers are mathematicians.

Algebra is the grammar that underlines the way that numbers work and within is contained the language that explains the patterns that lie behind the behaviour of numbers.

Physics is the application of maths, Physics formulas are simply algebraic codifications wherein Formulas represent solutions. Theory is Philosophy based on maths.

"Give me a place to stand and a lever long enough and using the moon as a fulcrum I will move the world!" - Archimedes

Music is a higher revelation than all wisdom and philosophy.

Music is the electric soil in which the spirit lives, thinks and invents – Ludwig Van Beethoven

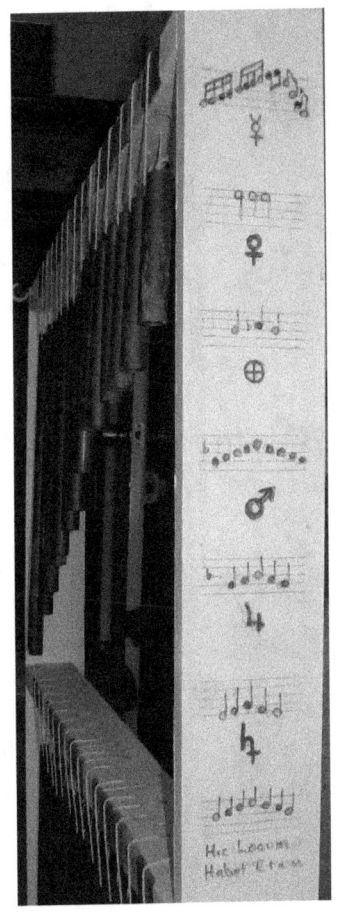

The Faerie gave humanity music

And when we play in their sacred places…they listen.

Nothing dies only changes form; nature wastes nothing.

Everything changes between states and forms and can change between states and forms simultaneously.

Everything seeks its centre

Everything serves its purpose

High goes to Low

Hot goes to Cold

Positive goes to Negative

Light goes to Dark

What goes Up must come Down

Between Positive and Negative Energy flows

Between Positive and Negative the light bulb is
illuminated.

Between Biology and Psyche Physiology exists

Between Cause and Effect Creation Occurs!

Child, how can I help you see?
Can I lend you my shoulders to stand on?
Now you see further than me, tell me what you see...

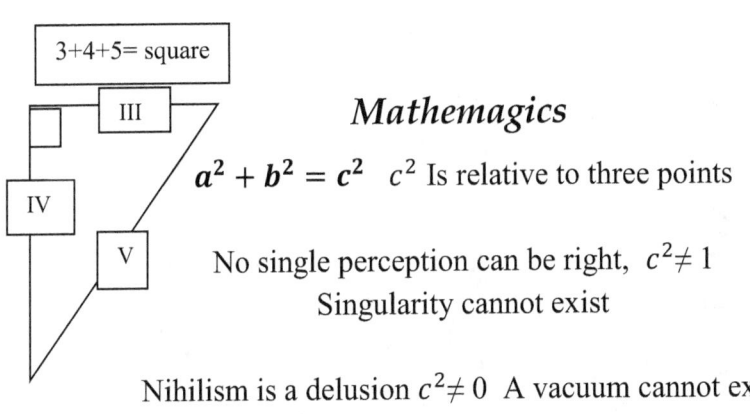

Mathemagics

$a^2 + b^2 = c^2$ c^2 Is relative to three points

No single perception can be right, $c^2 \neq 1$
Singularity cannot exist

Nihilism is a delusion $c^2 \neq 0$ A vacuum cannot exist

$2c \neq c^2$ Two wrongs do not make a right

Celerate F = ma   s = $^d/_t$.
Every action has an equal and opposite reaction

kE = $^1/_2$mv^2
Nothing rests, everything moves

Time is not wasted **E = mc^2** All is conserved
Everything is recorded in time and space

Celeratis
The speed of light is directly proportional to the speed of
an electromagnetic field **E = mφ**

Matter exist in 3 states relative to temperature and
pressure (Energy) **E^2 = Mφ^2**

71

Hermetic Wisdom

The All is in the mind, the Universe is mental

The Universe is mental held in the mind of The All.

All is in The All, and The All is in All.

Nothing rests everything moves, everything vibrates.

As above so below,

Everything is dual; everything has poles; everything has its pair of opposites; like and unlike are the same; opposites are identical in nature, but different in degree; extremes meet; all truths are but half truths; all paradoxes may be reconciled. Gender exists in everything

Everything flows, the pendulum swing to the left, is the pendulum swing to the right, rhythm compensates.

Cause and effect;

Mind may be transmuted from state to state;
Degree to degree; Condition to condition;
Pole to pole; Vibration to vibration.

The All is unknowable; reason must be treated with respect to the fundamental truth...

The All creates infinite universes

The truly wise, use law against laws,

Transmuting the unworthy to the worthy, Utilizing the higher against the lower.

Retrieved from the Public Domain

Modern Science

Modern science has become increasingly complex and specialised as its base of knowledge has grown. Due to the amount of accumulated information, no single person can hope to understand everything. For the sake of practicality science has become specialised into multiple disciplines. Each of these sciences and sub sciences has isolated itself from each other, each with its own language that hinders inter-scientific communication (LaViolette, 2004).

True Science has no belief. True science knows but three states of mind: denial, conviction, and the vast interval between the two, which is not belief, but the suspension of judgment. The harmony which geometry and mathematics, the only exact sciences, demonstrate to be the law of the Universe would be destroyed if evolution were perfectly exemplified in man alone and limited in the subordinate kingdoms. Harmony in the physical and mathematical world of sense is justice in the spiritual one. Justice produces harmony, harmony naturally invokes peace.

Through Divine Providence God accomplishes His will. To ensure that His purposes are fulfilled, God governs the affairs of men and works through the natural order of things. The laws of nature are nothing more than God's work in the Universe. The laws of nature have no inherent power; rather, they are the principles that God set in place to govern how things normally work. They are only "laws" because God decreed them.

I do not risk myself to explain anything; it is no business of mine. To authenticate simple facts, and maintain a truth which science desires to smother, is all I attempt to do. Nevertheless, I cannot resist the temptation to point out to those who would treat unjustly matters which resonate with the ordinary Laws of Physics.

In harmony with the divine spirit, nature, our Earth and everything pertaining to it enjoys a fertile period. The powers of plants, animals, and minerals magically sympathize with the "superior natures," and the divine soul of man is in perfect alliance with these "inferior" ones. But during the barren periods, the latter lose their magic sympathy, and the spiritual sight of the majority of mankind is so blinded as to lose every notion of the natural powers of its own divine spirit.

Willingly or not, all scientists must learn, through experience and their own errors, to suspend their judgment as to things which they have not been sufficiently experienced.

The only problem with scientific thinking is that it concludes its perception of reality to be reality itself

Truth remains one, and there is not a religion, science or philosophy that is not firmly built upon the rock of ages –

God, Creation and the Immortal Soul.

Esotoric Sciences

Esoteric Sciences are by nature eccentric;
As soon as they cease to be eccentric, they cease to be esoteric.
The study of the mage includes every branch of science; the
metaphysical as well as the physical, physiological, and
psychological in their common and esoteric phases.
The study of Alchemy is Universal, for it is both a physical
and a spiritual science. Therefore why doubt or wonder that

the ancients, who studied nature under its triune aspect, achieved discoveries which to our modern scientists appear unfathomable.

The indestructibility of mass and Energy being discovered and proven through the Law of conservation, the great problem of eternity is solved.

By the union of mass and Energy immortality is recognised. For people of science acquainted with the characteristics of Universal Energy, to maintain that life is merely a phenomenon of Energy, a species of matter, rather than a union and interaction between Mass and Energy, Earth and Environment, Body and Soul, amounts simply to a confession of his own incapability of analysing and properly understanding the Alpha and the Omega of even that – Mass and Energy

Willingly or not, all scientists shall learn, through experience and their own errors, to suspend their judgment as to things which they have not sufficiently examined so that the truth may reveal itself naturally of its own freewill. The lesson given to us all in this regard cannot be lost.

Let them push boldly on till they discover that it is not spirit that dwells in matter, but spirit which clings temporarily to matter; and that the advanced soul alone is an eternal, imperishable abode for all things visible and invisible. All knowledge, all arts are to be found in nature.

Descend first into the Earth then Ascend with the greatest sagacity from the Earth to Heaven, and then descend again to the Earth, and unite together the power of things inferior and superior; thus you will possess the light of the whole world, and all obscurity will fly away from you. This thing has more fortitude than fortitude itself, because it will overcome every subtle thing and penetrate every solid thing. By it the world was formed.

"The caterpillar becomes a butterfly, but the butterfly does not again return to the grub. Nature closes the door behind all that passes, and pushes life forward. Forms pass, consciousness remains, and does not recall that which it has once exhausted."

The Dove, The Rose and The Scepter

Since the Eighteenth and Nineteenth century scientists have scorned the metaphysical, spiritual side of life more and more; the alchemy of Francis Bacon's time becoming just basic chemistry, astrology being reduced to mechanical astronomy, gem atria being reduced to utilitarian cipher, living mathematics being turned into dead equations, and so on. Intellect has been adored, and the heart ignored – until recently, when scientists have penetrated so far into the workings of nature that they can no longer deny the metaphysical realities.

But Francis was at great pains to emphasise that Divinity – the Holy Wisdom or light pouring into the heart of a soul – is the principal part; and that Philosophy – the understanding aspect of the soul – is secondary to what is inspired from

78

God. In those days the soul was called the mind of man, and Francis pointed out over and over again that the soul or mind has two parts:

1, the heart that receives divine wisdom, and
2, the intellect that observes and analyses what the heart has been inspired with "from above' and the senses have registered from below, and then works out how to put the inspiration into action.

The imagination acts as a go-between, between heart and intellect as the handmaid to her royal mistress. But the two were needed; heart and intellect, inner and outer mind, princess and handmaid; and we should never forget the relationship between the two. Both together from the Bride (Philosophy) to the spirit (Divinity). Mankind should try to understand not just physical, but also metaphysical law, in fact, this was his prime object, and all should be done for Charity or Love.

Reference

Moore. Maree. (2004). The dove the rose and the sceptre – Retrieved from. Joshua books, Maroochydore BC, QLD Australia 4558

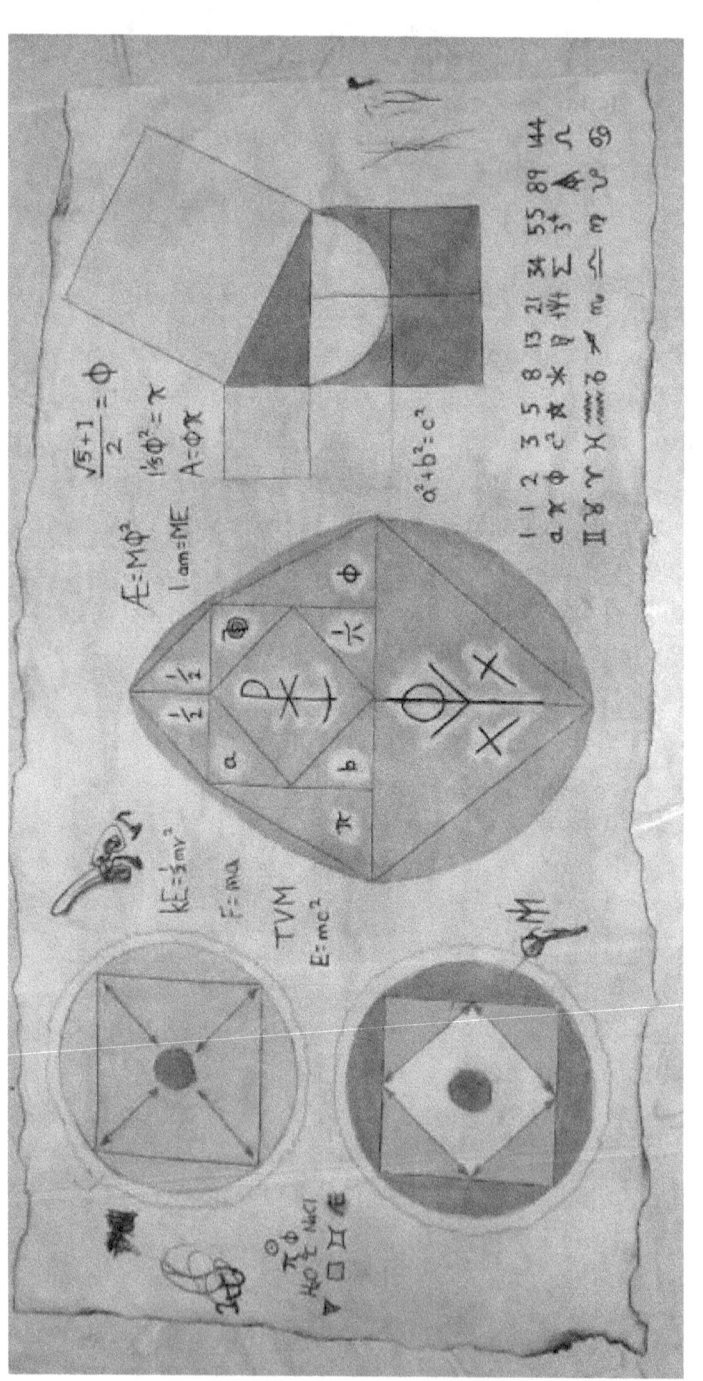

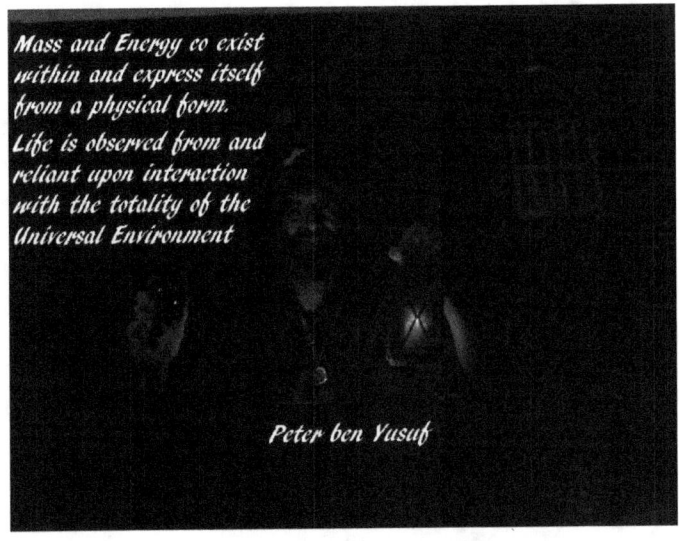

Mass and Energy co exist within and express itself from a physical form.
Life is observed from and reliant upon interaction with the totality of the Universal Environment

Peter ben Yusuf

It is what it is

Where in All Creation does Love not Exist
Does Love exist in truth
In truth does Love exist
If Love is all around us
and in all things too
Is it better to speak of love
or better to speak truth
Is love something that you say

Or something that you do
Poetry to ponder
a gift from me to you

The Valley

I sat upon the mountain top
And enjoyed the gracious view.
Yet realized while I sat there,
I spoiled the view for you.
I descended down as rivers flow,
As stream joins into stream
I coursed and winded my way along,
I remembered what I had seen
I made my way down into the valley,
For I was needed there.
The valley is now broken, no one seems to care,
That while they wish away their woes
And flush them all downstream
the mess that they leave behind someone has to clean.
When they descend once again
And pick up all their stuff
and complain about the mess and all this horrid muck
will they remember to make the change
Before climbing up again
or will they just rename apathy
With what is known as Zen

Epilogue

If a book claims to be inspired it must be tested.

It seems that in its study of the Created, mankind has lost the intelligence to recognize the existence of that of a Creator. Let alone the Creative Force that sparks the interest of mankind. To challenge my intellect with reason at this point in time is a difficult task.

As most information in this work was intuitively received, and not currently scientifically recognised, it has been a difficult topic to research and validate with regards to the worlds current attitude towards mathematical accuracy, physical and physiological aspects of being with respect to the word.

I hope I have presented a good science fiction, and I leave validation of information up to the reader and their application of Intelligence, Reason, Imagination, Contemplation and Discernment.

Thank you all kindly for sharing your perceptions, opinions, teachings, learning's and wisdom.

Wonder is the beginning of Wisdom

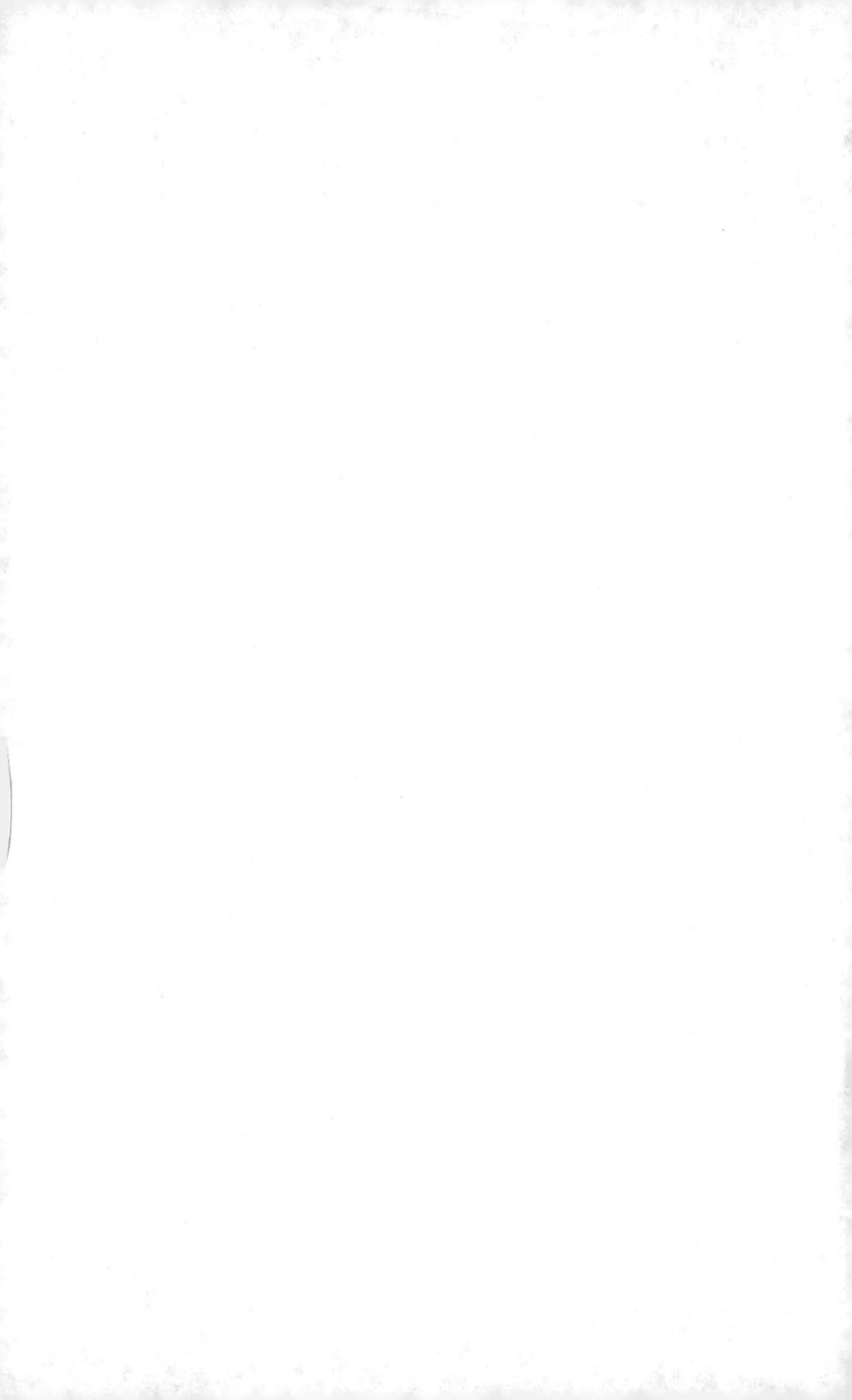

www.ingramcontent.com/pod-product-compliance
Lightning Source LLC
Chambersburg PA
CBHW062055280526
45788CB00003B/1235